'Where a spring rises or a river flows,
There ought we to build altars and offer sacrifices.'
Seneca

This edition © Wooden Books Ltd 2000
First published as *Holy Wells in Great Britain* 2000 AD

Published by Wooden Books Ltd.
Glastonbury, Somerset

British Library Cataloguing in Publication Data
Martin, C. J.
Sacred Springs

A CIP catalogue record for this important book
is available from the British Library

ISBN 1 904263 45 3

Printed on 100% FSC approved sustainable papers
by RR Donnelley Asia Printing Solutions Ltd.

SACRED
SPRINGS

written and illustrated by

Christina Martin

This book is dedicated to Mike and to Jayne.

*With thanks to Morag Young, Jo Elkins,
Alison McClean and the staff at Parbold Library.*

Further reading: Fentynyow Kernow, in search of Cornwall's Holy Wells *by Cheryl Straffon,* The Living Stream *by James Rattue,* Holy Wells of Bath and Bristol Region *by Phil Quinn,* The Holy Wells of Wales *by Francis Jones and* The Holy Wells of Ireland *by Patrick Logan.*

Above: St Michael's Well, Bolton-le-Sands, Lancashire.
Front page: Head from St Ambrusca's Well, Cornwall.
Title page: St Patrick's Well, Heysham, Lancashire.

CONTENTS

The Monk's Well, Edington, Wiltshire

INTRODUCTION

What we now call holy wells are those springs and wells that, through time, have become associated with a particular healing ability, those associated with saints or other individuals, or those treated with particular veneration for their spiritually uplifting qualities. The fascination of holy wells lies in the stories that have grown up around them, and their beauty and atmosphere.

Evidence of water worship exists worldwide and settlements have been situated by springs for thousands of years. Long ago water was seen as the abode of gods and spirits, as seen at COVENTINA'S WELL at Carrawburgh, where a Celtic goddess of wells and springs was worshipped in a Roman temple complex. Later on, Christian missionaries often established a cell by a sacred spring and the saint's name would then attach to the well, such as happened at ST SEIRIOL'S WELL on Anglesey. The wells were often considered most potent on the saint's day with which they were associated and great pilgrimages occurred on those days.

Holy wells are often situated by churches and chapels, which made use of their water both to heal and to baptise. These wells have often been cared for because of this, but many others are now dry, or overgrown and lost, remembered only in street names. Conduits and pumps were later developments which received the same veneration for bringing water to isolated areas, and in the mid-eighteenth century visiting spas became fashionable, with their scientifically proven qualities. Other wells may be just a natural, clear spring through to the ornate majesty of the medieval well house of ST WINEFRIDE'S WELL, North Wales (*see page 46*). Some holy wells have been fated to eventually supply their healing water to a cattle trough, which has happened to ST CANDIDA'S WELL, in Dorset.

There are many fascinating legends attached to holy wells, and spirits and fairies are not always far away. Some wells are haunted by white ladies or ghosts, as seen in Lancashire at PEG O' NELL'S WELL, which is haunted by a servant who died there. She died whilst fetching water from the well, when her master wished that she might fall and break her neck. Some spirits are benign, but others are malicious and must be appeased by the performance of a particular ritual at the well. Peg is seen as an evil spirit, who claims a victim every seven years by causing them to drown.

Certain trees with particular significance were often planted by wells. Rags were hung in their branches (*see* MADRON WELL, *page 6*) but various items might be pushed into the bark, such as coins, nails or pins. Queen Victoria is said to have placed a silver coin for luck in the tree beside ST MOURIE'S WELL, on Loch Maree. After years of pilgrims following this tradition the tree finally died. It can also be noted that particular types of tree may be found by wells, such as hazel trees (which were the Celtic tree of knowledge), thorn trees, oak, ash and yew. Irish mythology tells of CONNLA'S WELL, where nine hazel trees stood as guardians above the well. Each tree dropped a nut into the water that was then eaten by a salmon, which in so doing acquired all the knowledge of the world.

In the past pilgrims left many different offerings at the wells and a variety of rituals were followed when the water was used for divination, or for healing a particular condition. For example, at certain wells warts were cured by being bathed then pricked with a pin, which was then bent and thrown in the water. It is not known why the pins were bent, though it has been suggested that it was to exorcise the evil spirit thought to occupy the person. Pins were also left at wells related to childbirth and fertility. Nowadays many offerings are still left, and respect is seen in the formal Derbyshire well-dressing ceremonies, which give thanks for the gift of water, and in the degenerated form of the wishing well, where we cast a coin in the water to catch the good fortune given by the well.

With chemically cleaned water now pumped to our homes at the turn of a tap it is easy to forget the natural reaction to seeing a crystal-clear spring of pure water bubbling out of the ground, cold and refreshing. But Britain's holy wells have been more than just a source of clean water, it is the qualities of that water with their magical abilities to heal, to make fertile, to predict the future, to baptise and even to curse that make them unique. This book tells some of the fascinating stories that surround the wells, and shows the variety of delightful sites to be discovered.

Old prints of Cornish holy wells, c.1870: Dupath Well, near Callington; St. Dominick's Holy Well; Laneast Holy Well.

CONDITIONS & CURES
the healing powers of holy waters

The waters of holy wells have long been used to heal many conditions, by drinking, bathing or occasionally applying in a poultice. Sometimes their names reflect what they healed, such as the Eye Well, Wart Well and Gout Well.

The variety of conditions healed was vast. Anything from broken bones, lameness, ruptures, sprains and rheumatism to deafness, headaches, asthma, tumours, jaundice and infertility. Children could be healed of whooping cough and rickets. The greatest number of wells healed eyes; at Roman Wroxeter forty plaster eyes were found, plus one of sheet gold. The healing of the 'eye' may be identified with the healing of the soul.

Animals could be cured at some wells. However, at others, if an animal were put in the water this would deprive the well of its power to heal. At a well in Wales a dead dog was placed in the water and, because of this insult, the spring ceased to flow.

Perhaps the most unusual treatments were seen for the cure of mental illnesses at the bowsening pools, as seen at ST CLEER'S WELL in Cornwall (*illustrated opposite*). Here the unfortunate patient would be thrown backwards into the cold well water, plunged up and down vigorously, then taken to the church and prayed over. If they did not regain their wits the process would be repeated until it showed signs of success. It was obviously an alarming example of an early form of shock treatment.

MADRON WELL
West Penwith, Cornwall

Just northwest of Penzance, the small village of Madron has one of the most famous wells in Cornwall, found at the end of an atmospheric wooded pathway.

A *rag bush* marks the well. This is a tree hung with many colourful scraps of cloth left by visitors, and these can be seen at many wells. In the past, a pilgrim seeking healing would soak a rag from their clothing in the water and tie it to the tree. As the rag rotted away, so their disease would leave them.

Nearby is a pretty ruined baptistry, where the clear water from the well runs into one corner. Children brought for healing were dipped in the well three times, then taken round it sunwise, east to west, nine times. The number of times an action must be performed was very significant (*see page 52*).

Madron is also a well used for divination. In this instance, maidens would float a straw cross on the water to tell when they would marry (*see too page 44*). The water of holy wells could be usefully consulted to divine how long a person might live, what the weather would be or even if husbands were faithful.

> NEARBY: *Nearby is the delightful* SANCREED HOLY WELL, *which is also marked by a rag bush, and* NANCEGLOS WELL, *near the entrance to Trenwainton Gardens. On the magical St Michael's Mount is the* GIANT'S WELL, *said to be where the giant Cormoran died, which is also known as* JACK THE GIANT KILLER'S WELL.

St Levan's Well
West Penwith, Cornwall

ST LEVAN'S WELL is set in a high, dramatic location, on the cliffs overlooking Porthchapel beach where the turquoise waves crash against the shore.

St Levan would walk the clifftops, his path marked by a brighter shade of green than the surrounding grass. He was a fisherman and would take one fish a day from the sea. One day he caught a chad, which is the fry of the red bream, but felt it was too small and threw it back. Again he caught the small fish, and again threw it back. When he caught it for a third time he thought Providence had provided it, and took it to feed his sister and niece. But unfortunately the child choked on her first mouthful, and this he saw as a punishment for his dissatisfaction. From then on, the fishermen called the chad 'chuck-cheeld', meaning choke child.

Above the well, in the churchyard, is a large ancient stone, split in two by a blow from St Levan's fist. He prophesied that when the day came a pack horse with panniers could pass through the stone, the world would end. A number of wells are situated near megaliths and stone circles.

NEARBY: *Nearby is the peaceful* ALSIA WELL, *famed for healing weak and rickety children. There are also two wells at* CHAPEL EUNY *possessing powerful healing waters, which lie near to the Carn Euny Iron Age village.*

ST AUGUSTINE'S WELL
Cerne Abbas, Dorset

Peaceful ST AUGUSTINE'S WELL is situated near the abbey ruins below the most famous hill figure in Britain, the Cerne Abbas giant (*illustrated*). His presence is a potent symbol of fertility above the surrounding rich countryside. The water of the well was used to cure general illness and sore eyes.

The well was also known as the SILVER WELL, with pagan origins, a place where silver might be thrown as an offering. Its name may also describe the appearance of the water.

A legend tells that St Augustine travelled to Cerne and struck his staff to the ground in the valley below the giant. Here a miraculous spring gushed forth, a common story at wells.

Many holy wells have particular rituals for drinking their water to ensure the effectiveness of the cure. At this well the water must be drunk from a laurel leaf, whilst looking towards the church and away from the giant. At other wells different vessels must be used, such as a limpet shell at ST GOVAN'S WELL, Wales, or even, rather alarmingly, a skull. The skull links wells to heads (*see too page 46*).

NEARBY: *Another powerful healing well in Dorset is near* UPWEY CHURCH. *As at St Augustine's Well, the water is drunk from a laurel leaf and then a wish is made. To the west, near the pretty seaside town of Lyme Regis, are the waters of* ST CANDIDA'S WELL *at Morcombelake, once used to cure eye troubles.*

CHALICE WELL
Glastonbury, Somerset

The **CHALICE WELL** is found in the peaceful Chalice Well Gardens at the foot of Chalice Hill. This area is dominated by the imposing presence of Glastonbury Tor, the ancient and sacred Isle of Avalon.

Tradition says that long ago Joseph of Arimathea travelled to England bringing the Holy Grail, the chalice used by Christ at the Last Supper. The chalice was hidden in the well, and later was sought by King Arthur's knights as a sacred quest.

The red iron-rich water gives another name, **THE BLOOD SPRING**. Tradition says the water is coloured by Christ's blood, caught in the Holy Grail at the crucifixion. The lid of Chalice Well is decorated with the mystical *vesica piscis* (vessel of the fish) produced by two overlapping circles. The design was created by Frederick Bligh Bond who excavated the nearby abbey where the grave of King Arthur and Queen Guinevere can be seen.

From beneath the Tor flows **THE WHITE SPRING** and, in the past, the red and white waters merged together, flowing into the abbey grounds. Here **ST JOSEPH'S WELL** can be found in a niche in the south wall of the Lady Chapel.

NEARBY: *At Wells, by the magnificent cathedral, may be seen* **ST ANDREW'S WELL**, *once known as the* **BOTTOMLESS WELL**. *Near the atmospheric church at Doulting is* **ST ALDHELM'S WELL** *with its now neglected long trough, probably once used as a bath for pilgrims.*

13

THE HOT SPRINGS
Bath, Somerset

The steaming HOT SPRINGS OF BATH can be seen in the impressive Roman Bath Museum, in the centre of the elegant city.

Although visited long before Roman times, what we see today are the remains of an extensive Roman temple and bath complex. The iron-rich water stains surrounding stonework orange and flows at 250,000 gallons a day with a constant temperature of 46°C.

Tradition says that King Bladud, father of King Lear, discovered its curative powers whilst living as a lowly swineherd. He had leprosy, and noticed that the pigs, who had also contracted it, were cured by wallowing in the mud of the Hot Spring. In the museum there is a carved head that may represent King Bladud as a solar deity, though it is also sometimes identified as Medusa.

The Celtic goddess of the Hot Spring was Sulis, who the Romans identified with Minerva. The city was named Aquae Sulis, and the temple dedicated to Sulis-Minerva.

The Romans left many offerings to the gods, chiefly coins, showing the link to wishing wells. The spring was also used for cursing, to invoke retribution on an enemy. Curses, inscribed on stones or lead sheets, were cast in the water.

> NEARBY: *Nearby is the handsome* MONK'S WELL *at Monkton Farleigh, and the fern-lined basins of the* HOLY WELL OF CONKWELL, *near Winsley, where wishes can be made while drinking its water.*

15

DANIEL'S WELL
and the Swallowhead Spring, Wiltshire

The ancient hill town of Malmesbury stands on a rocky eminence, almost completely surrounded by rivers and noted for its magnificent abbey church.

Below the abbey rises DANIEL'S WELL, a clear spring which flows into a pool. This is named after Bishop Daniel of Malmesbury who submerged his body in the cold waters throughout the year as a penance.

This story relates to traditions at other wells. It is said that at ST CHAD'S WELL, Lichfield, the saint would go naked to stand in the water and pray. St Aldhelm is said to have sat in his well at Doulting singing psalms, and St Patrick sat naked in the STRUEL WELLS, County Down, singing spiritual songs.

Many houses in the old part of Malmesbury have wells. One private home hides another of ST ALDHELM'S HOLY WELLS, where the saint is said to have meditated. Legend says that small fishes magically appear from nowhere and just as mysteriously disappear.

NEARBY: *Not to be missed is the* SWALLOWHEAD SPRING *(illustrated), the source of the River Kennet. It is tucked quietly in the amazing Avebury landscape overlooked by the mysterious Silbury Hill and much visited and decorated. Other wells in Wiltshire include the large* DIPPING WELL *in the centre of Market Lavington and the delightfully peaceful well at Edington, known as the* MONK'S WELL *(see opposite page 1), which is hidden away from the main road.*

SEVEN WELLS
Bisley, Gloucestershire

The peaceful and picturesque village of Bisley stands high on the Cotswold Hills and the delightful well house is to the south of the church.

Rev. Thomas Keble restored the wells in 1863, and introduced the custom of well dressing on Ascension Day. This well is one of the growing number of wells to be decorated in this way.

The well house ranks as one of the most attractive and unusual in Britain. The ornate semi-circular structure has five spouts of water issuing into the trough. At either end two more spouts flow, bringing the total to seven. Seven is a sacred number and often occurs in rituals at wells. Above the wells is an inscription:

'O YE WELLS, BLESS YE THE LORD: PRAISE
HIM AND MAGNIFY HIM FOREVER.'

There is also an unusual well-cross in the churchyard above, which in one tradition is identified as a lantern or *poor souls' light*. It is said that the well below was filled in after a priest fell down it and drowned. The rather gruesome name for this handsome monument is the Bonehouse.

NEARBY: LADY'S WELL at Hempsted, near Gloucester, has a well chapel with a fine position overlooking the Severn and, further west, ST ANTHONY'S WELL, near Micheldean, has a large bathing pool used for curing skin diseases.

ST MARGARET'S WELL
Binsey, Oxfordshire

ST MARGARET'S WELL is found in Binsey churchyard, across Port Meadow, the marshy common land northwest of Oxford.

A legend tells that St Frideswide was pursued here by an unwelcome suitor, King Algar. He was struck blind for his boldness, but St Frideswide prayed to St Margaret and a miraculous spring rose from the ground. She used the water to cure his blindness, and founded an oratory where pilgrims subsequently came for healing. The prayers of saints have often brought forth healing water (*see also* ST HILDA'S WELL, *page 36*).

St Frideswide's legend is illustrated in the beautiful Burne-Jones stained glass window glowing with rich colours in Christ Church, Oxford, which shows sixteen scenes from her life.

More recently, the well has become famous for a different reason: it is the original TREACLE WELL mentioned in the curious tale told by the Dormouse in *Alice in Wonderland* by Lewis Carroll. It is interesting to note that in medieval times 'treacle' was a healing fluid, an antidote to poisoning.

> NEARBY: *To the northwest may be found* FAIR ROSAMOND'S WELL, *in the beautiful setting of Blenheim Park, and the* LADY'S WELL AT WILCOTE *is found in Wychwood Forest. On the other side of Oxford is* ST BARTHOLOMEW'S WELL, *in the churchyard at Cowley. The taking of its waters would allow the penitent forty days less in Purgatory, before they finally reached heaven.*

St Ann's Well & Holy Well
Malvern, Hereford and Worcester

The distinctive building of the HOLY WELL is situated at MALVERN WELLS, with ST ANN'S WELL near Great Malvern. Their waters were used for treating many infirmities.

Used as healing wells from an early date, in the eighteenth century Dr John Wall established the town as a spa, building accommodation and a bathhouse. In the early days donkeys carried the patients up to the wells. The notable quality of the water is its purity—it has no taste. This was celebrated in a cheerful rhyme of the time:

> *"The Malvern water," says Dr Wall,*
> *"Is famed for containing just nothing at all."*

Later it became a centre for hydrotherapy, involving elaborate and not entirely pleasant water treatments. A visitor, coming to recover from stress, could expect to start the morning by being wrapped in a cold wet sheet, then further wrapped with blankets, staying encased this way for an hour. After this cold water was poured over them. Most apparently did well on this therapy.

NEARBY: *Wells dedicated to St Ethelbert may be found in historic* HEREFORD *near the cathedral and at nearby* MARDEN *under the church. The saint was murdered and both springs originate where his body was rested. At Romsley Church, in the beautiful Clent Hills is* ST KENELM'S WELL. *In this case the spring rose where the murdered body of young King Kenelm was buried.*

SPAS
centres for water treatment

Often starting as recognised holy wells and springs, the spas of Britain developed at the end of the seventeenth century, reached popular heights in the middle of the eighteenth century and are still a very active industry today. The spas (or *spaws* as they were also known) were health resorts where the waters had proven mineral content and therapeutic value. The waters were chiefly iron bearing ('chalybeate'), sulphurous, effervescent or saline. Sometimes an area possessed a variety of waters, each used to cure specific conditions.

At their height spas were visited not only for their waters and fresh country air, but also for the lively social life of gaming houses, inns, music and dancing which they offered.

Many spas closed as the Health Service developed but there are hopes some may yet be revived. DROITWICH SPA is still being used for its original purpose. The saturated brine waters are rivalled only by the Dead Sea and are used for weightless bathing, which is particularly effective for rheumatic conditions.

SPA TOWNS *to visit, where the waters may still be sampled, include elegant* ROYAL TUNBRIDGE WELLS, *with its handsome Pantiles area,* HARROGATE, STRATHPEFFER, ROYAL LEAMINGTON SPA, BUXTON, *historic* BATH *and* MALVERN. *At* CHELTENHAM *the quality of the spring water was recognised because of all the healthy pigeons in the area. The earlier name of the spa town of* LLANDRINDOD WELLS *was ffynnon llwyn y gog, meaning 'the well in the cuckoo's grove'.*

THE WIZARD'S WELL
Alderley Edge, Cheshire

The mysterious WIZARD'S WELL is located on mystical Alderley Edge and overlooks the vast expanse of the Cheshire plain.

The stone trough of the well is situated under a damp rocky overhang. Above it is carved an enigmatic face, and the words:

'Drink of this and take thy fill
For the water falls by the wizard's will.'

The legend tells of a farmer returning from Macclesfield market, where he had been unable to sell his pure white horse. A hooded old man approached him and led him to a rock face where two gates opened at his command. Inside were many warriors asleep with their white horses. The old man said that they needed one more horse, and were willing to pay gold for it. The warriors were waiting for the country to be in need, he said, when they would wake and ride out. The farmer then found himself back out in the darkness, loaded with the gold coins he had been given. No one has been able to find the gates since.

The old man, or wizard, has often been identified with Merlin, and the sleeping warriors with King Arthur and his knights, waiting to return.

NEARBY: *To the west are the isolated* ST PLEGMUND'S WELL *at Plemstall, near Mickle Trafford, sadly dry but with rags and shells left as offerings, and boggy* ST OSWALD'S WELL *at Winwick, Warrington.*

LADYEWELL
Fernyhalgh, Lancashire

Situated to the north of Preston, the attractive LADYEWELL at Fernyhalgh is a healing and pilgrimage shrine to this day.

The legend of its discovery concerns a seafaring Irish merchant who, journeying home, was caught in a fierce storm.

Praying to God, he vowed that if he were saved he would perform a pious deed. When finally washed onto the Lancashire shore, a voice told him to find a crabtree at Fernyhalgh and there build a chapel. He searched the area, but was unable to find the place at all. Later, returning to where he was staying, he heard that the maid there was out looking for a lost cow. When she returned, he heard that the cow had been found at Fernyhalgh. So he asked the maid to direct him and there he found an undiscovered statue of the Virgin Mary, the spring and an unusual crabtree that had coreless fruit. Here he built his shrine.

> NEARBY: *Slightly further to the north is the CHURCH WELL in a recess near the Heysham church, and ST MICHAEL'S WELL at Bolton-le-Sands, a beautiful, clear and bubbling spring which is carefully tended. To the south is the recently restored STANDISH WELL, and the enigmatic HIC-BIBI WELL, hidden in undergrowth near Coppull.*

St Oswald's Well
Kirkoswald, Cumbria

Kirkoswald is a small picturesque village in the Eden Valley, northeast of Penrith. The village derives its name from the Church of St Oswald, and ST OSWALD'S WELL is on the side of the church.

The church has actually been built over the spring, which passes under the full length of the nave. The water emerges in the carefully preserved well house at the side. Many churches, minsters and cathedrals were sited over springs.

As a drinking well, also used for baptism and pilgrimage, it is a now rare example of a well with a drinking cup on a chain for tasting its clear waters (*see also* SCOTLANDWELL, *page 48*).

To the south, near the church at Edenhall, is overgrown ST CUTHBERT'S WELL, on private land. This well is linked to a relic called a *Luck*, said to bring good fortune to its guardian. The Edenhall Luck was a beautiful, richly coloured glass chalice, and fairies seen dancing round it were heard to sing:

'*If this glass should break or fall, Farewell the Luck of Edenhall.*'

A special case was made to protect the Luck and it is now in the Victoria and Albert Museum, London.

NEARBY: *Also in Cumbria is the dipping pool of* ST HELEN'S WELL *at Great Ashby, said never to fail, and there is a handsome well house at* ST PATRICK'S WELL *at the head of breathtaking Lake Ullswater. Another well beneath a church is* ST PATRICK'S WELL *at Aspatria.*

ST ANN'S WELL
Buxton, Derbyshire

ST ANN'S WELL is found in the centre of Buxton, the highest town in England, set in the beautiful Derbyshire hills. Buxton's springs were known as one of the Seven Wonders of the Peak.

St Ann's Well takes its name from the mother of the Virgin Mary, who was responsible for miracles of healing. The Romans used the water, as it is a natural thermal spring, though not as hot as the waters at Bath. They named the town *Aquae Arnemetiae* or 'Waters of the Goddess of the Grove', taking the name from the minor Celtic deity, Arnemetia.

In the eighteenth century the Crescent was erected on the site of the original Roman baths, and Buxton became a thriving spa town. Later additions included a Pump Room, renamed 'St Ann's Well' when refurbished in 1912. This attractive building is occasionally accessible at the base of the Slopes. It has a sunken marble well from which water would be dispensed up to the semicircular balcony by an assistant. Next to this building is an ever-flowing pump of water, inscribed '*A Well of Living Waters*'.

> NEARBY: *There are many wells in nearby villages – beautiful* TISSINGTON *with its six delightful, clear wells and Eyam with* MOMPESSON'S WELL, *used as an exchange point for food and money at the time of the Great Plague. Also, there is Ashford-in-the-Water with its* SHEEPWASH WELL *and pumps,* STONEY MIDDLETON *with its warm springs and the wells of bustling* BAKEWELL.

WELL DRESSING
an ancient custom

The ancient art of well dressing originates from early veneration of the spirit of the spring, bringing fertility to the land. The Romans introduced the festival of Fontinalia, dedicated to Fontus, the god of springs, where garlands adorned wells and streams. The early church saw this custom as water worship, and sporadically discouraged the practice, often rededicating wells to a saint. However the tradition slowly returned: Tissington in Derbyshire revived it to celebrate the village escaping the Black Death in 1349. Other villages used well dressing as thanks for the provision of piped water, decorating the taps and pumps.

The practice now takes a Christianised form with services and blessings. An elaborate, brightly-coloured picture is produced, usually of a biblical subject. The picture is made from natural materials such as petals, leaves, moss, bark and cones, which create the colours and outlines of the picture. They are pressed into wet clay that has been prepared on special large boards. The picture develops from the bottom upwards, with petals overlapping one another to allow rainwater to run off. Much hard work and skill go into creating these beautiful mosaic-like pictures, which then go on show for about a week.

> **WELL DRESSING CELEBRATIONS** *are seen mainly in Derbyshire from May to September.* **BUXTON** *holds its ceremony in July,* **EYAM** *in late August and the picturesque village of* **TISSINGTON** *in early June. In recent years, however, the custom has been spreading to an ever-growing number of places, such as* **MALVERN**.

St Hilda's Well
Hinderwell, North Yorkshire

Northwest of the delightful harbour town of Whitby is the quiet village of Hinderwell, with its churchyard well.

The village name commemorates Hilda, abbess of Whitby. Legend tells that the illustrious saint was travelling to Guisborough when, exhausted and thirsty, she prayed, and the spring arose at that spot. Its pure, clear water possessed healing qualities and to mark the miracle a church was built.

The restored ST HILDA'S WELL is reached down a flight of stone steps. On Ascension Day, people would visit the well with liquorice, which would be mixed with the water and drunk. This was also known as Spanish Water Day. This is a custom seen at many wells, where sugar, liquorice, peppermint or brown sugar was added to well water as a sweetener.

> NEARBY: *Two unusual Yorkshire wells are the amazing* PETRIFYING WELL *at Knaresborough, with its ability to turn anything to stone and* THE EBBING AND FLOWING WELL *at Giggleswick. Legend tells of a terrified nymph who was pursued by a satyr till the gods, answering her prayers, turned her into a crystal-clear healing spring. And so the water ebbs and flows with her breath.* ST CHAD'S WELL *and* ST CEDD'S WELL *are nearby to Lastingham church, with its atmospheric crypt. St Chad was St Cedd's brother and is the patron saint of wells.*

HOLY WELLS, WALSINGHAM
Little Walsingham, Norfolk

Situated to the north of Fakenham is the small pretty village of Little Walsingham. Its holy wells are the most visited of all those in England.

In 1061 the widow Richeldis de Faverches had a miraculous vision of the Virgin Mary, who showed her the house of the Annunciation and told her to build an exact replica. The vision occurred near two holy wells. A wooden holy house was built here, which then became a pilgrimage site of great importance.

After the Reformation, the wells degenerated into wishing wells, though still with a strict ritual. The visitor knelt his bare right knee on the stone between the two wells, then plunged his hands in the water. A wish was made, and the water drunk. The wish would be fulfilled within a year if it were never told.

In 1931 an Anglican shrine was built housing a replica of the holy house and at this time another well was discovered, fed by the two holy wells nearby in the abbey grounds. Today's pilgrims visit this holy place, and use this well for blessing and healing.

> NEARBY: *Nearby wells to visit are* ST WITHBURGA'S WELL *in St Nicholas' churchyard, East Dereham, and the quirky* ST WALSTAN'S WELL *at Bawburgh, looking exactly like a typical story-book wishing well, but once a revered place of pilgrimage.*

HOLY WELL OF ST MARY'S
Willesden, London

The HOLY WELL OF ST MARY'S in bustling Willesden is found within the peace of the church, rising in a pump.

This is another well that rises under a church (*see also St Oswald's Well, page 30*). The poet Sir John Betjeman is known to have used the water for its healing qualities.

This pilgrimage site is unique because of its association with a statue of the Black Virgin. The original was burnt, as were so many others, at the Reformation, but it was replaced in 1972 by a new one beautifully carved from black limewood.

While London does not appear to be the most obvious place to find holy wells there were many at one time. The River Fleet, now covered by roads and buildings around Fleet Street, was also known as the 'River of Wells', and place names such as Clerkenwell remind us of their presence. Sadlers Wells opera house is built over the site of the holy well of St John's Priory, and later named after Thomas Sadler who uncovered it and turned it into a successful spa.

> NEARBY: *Some of the most famous London wells are buried under railway stations—*ST CHAD'S WELL *was lost when the Metropolitan Railway was built,* BAGNIGGE WELLS *is under busy Kings Cross station and neighbouring* PANCRAS WELLS *is under St Pancras Station. However, there is still an ornate nineteenth century fountain in Well Walk, marking the site of the famous* HAMPSTEAD SPA.

St Govan's Well
Bosherston, Dyfed

ST GOVAN'S WELL and its isolated chapel can be found in the breathtaking coastal scenery at St Govan's Head, south of Bosherston near Pembroke. It was famous for curing lameness, rheumatism and eye troubles.

The well and chapel are squeezed in a crevice, led down to by steep steps which are reputedly uncountable. Long ago pirates stole the silver chapel bell but sea nymphs rescued it and hid it in a rock, which rang if struck. In the chapel there is a magical niche where the rock opened to hide St Govan when enemies pursued him. Rib-like impressions can be seen where his body is said to have touched the sides. Turning round in this niche is said to be lucky.

This was a popular healing well where traditionally water was drunk from a limpet shell (*see also* ST AUGUSTINE'S WELL, *page 10*). A legend says that St Govan was actually King Arthur's nephew, Sir Gawain, who came here to live as a hermit.

NEARBY: *Other wells to visit in this area are* ST ANTHONY'S WELL, *below Llanstephan Castle's mound, and* ST MARY'S WELL *at Maenclochog. This well is situated near the remains of a cromlech which, if struck, would ring until water from the well was taken to the church. Further west is the atmospheric* ST NON'S WELL *near St Davids, the place where St Non gave birth to St David.*

St Cybi's Well
Llangybi, Gwynedd

St Cybi's Well is found beyond the churchyard in the delightful small village of Llangybi, with beautiful views across Snowdonia.

The isolated well consists of a well building plus a custodian's cottage, all now in a ruined state. It is an interesting example of a holy well that possessed a *guardian*, in this instance an eel. The visitor to the well would stand in the water and, if the eel wrapped itself round their legs, it was believed that they would be cured. The eel was removed on one occasion, and local people believed the water lost its power.

The guardian acted as an oracle, its actions predicted the future or foretold the success of the cure. They included sacred fishes, such as trout and salmon, but the most unusual was a guardian fly, at St Michael's Well, Kirkmichael in Scotland. On occasions, it was said, the fly might appear to be dead, but it was resurrected each time and lived on.

St Cybi's Well was also used for love divination. Usually if a handkerchief set on the water sank the relationship would end, if it floated the love was true.

> NEARBY: *To the north is* Beuno's Well *near the magnificent church at Clynnog Fawr. Scraping stone dust from the saint's chapel and adding it to the well water would cure sore eyes (see page 4). On Anglesey behind Penmon Priory is* St Seirol's Well, *with its crystal clear water in a neat well house tucked against a cliff.*

ST WINEFRIDE'S WELL
Holywell, Clwyd

ST WINEFRIDE'S WELL with its bubbling, clear water is housed in a handsome medieval well chapel in the town of Holywell, also known as the 'Lourdes of Wales'. It is a much visited pilgrimage site, its water used for drinking and bathing. People cured by its water left their crutches and sticks as a sign of its healing power.

This is the most notable example of the widespread theme of a well rising where a severed head fell. The legend here tells of Prince Caradoc who, spurned by Winefride, took a sword and beheaded her. Where her head fell a spring gushed up. Her uncle, St Beuno, cursed the prince who was immediately swallowed up by the earth. Beuno then replaced Winefride's head and restored her to life. Statues show the thin cut line round her neck which she bore for the rest of her life.

This legend links heads with water sources. At some wells a skull was traditionally used as a drinking cup, in others severed heads were washed, another variation on the theme (*see page 50*).

NEARBY: *Near to St Winefrides's Well is* BEUNO'S WELL, Tremeirchion, *where water flows out through the mouth of a strange carved head, and* ST DYFNOG'S WELL, *hidden in the peaceful wood behind Llanrhaeadr church with its impressive stained glass. Further west is the* HOLY WELL OF ST CELYNIN, *high above the Conwy valley, by the quiet, isolated church of Llangelynin, near Henryd.*

SCOTLANDWELL
near Kinross, Scotland

SCOTLANDWELL is found to the west of Kinross and the elegant well is in the centre of the village.

The Romans passed through this area, and drank from the bubbling, pure water. Afterwards they named the well *Fons Scotiae*—the well of Scotland, and so gave the name to the village also.

A very ancient well, the water was used to heal the sick at the thirteenth century hospital of the Red Friars and is also credited with curing Robert the Bruce, King of Scotland, of his leprosy.

The well house is a wooden structure which covers the large rectangular well trough, from which the water flows. The present structure is a reconstruction, dated 1858. A metal cup hangs by a chain, inviting visitors to sample the crystal-clear water.

> NEARBY: *Not far away are* ST FILLAN'S WELL *at Aberdour on the Firth of Forth, and another sacred* ST FILLAN'S WELL *at Pittenweem ('place of the cave'), further to the northeast. In the seventh century St Fillan lived in this cave, using a stone shelf for a bed and drinking from the well, the cave's pure spring. Later his abode became a shrine tended by monks of Pittenweem Priory, and even later it was used by eighteenth century smugglers. To the south, in Holyrood Park in Edinburgh is* ST MARGARET'S WELL, *near the ruins of St Anthony's Chapel, with splendid views over the city.*

49

WELL OF THE HEADS
Invergarry, Inverness, Scotland

The unusual monument over the WELL OF THE HEADS is found on the road south of Invergarry, beside attractive Loch Oich.

A hand holding seven severed heads and a dirk (a dagger worn by Highlanders) surmounts the monument. It commemorates the revenge killing of the murderers of two young brothers, Ranald and Alexander McDonald. The seven men were hunted, killed and beheaded. Their heads were then washed in the well before being taken to Invergarry castle, as proof that they were dead. A different version of the story says that the heads were cooled in the water because their teeth were gnashing with rage.

Celtic folklore is rich with stories involving the cutting off of heads, and well water often gushes out of the mouth of a carved face. A similar tradition persists in the mysterious figure of the Green Man, from whose head grows rich curling foliage.

> NEARBY: *Nearby wells include* ST IGNATIUS' WELL *at Glassburn, and* ST MARY'S WELL *in Culloden wood. This latter is also known as the* BLUE WELL, *or* WELL OF YOUTH, *and tradition says the water is turned to wine on 1ˢᵗ May. This was a great pilgrimage site, but later gatherings became rather riotous. There is also the rock-hewn* HOLY WELL *at Burghead, and the incredible* CLOUTIE WELL *at Munlochy, where thousands of colourful rags hang on lines between the trees by the well.*

STRUEL WELLS
Downpatrick, Co. Down, Ireland

The ancient town of Downpatrick is south of Belfast, and to the east of the town can be found ST PATRICK'S WELLS at Struel, consisting of the EYE WELL, DRINKING WELL and two bath houses.

Pilgrimages are also known as *patterns* or *patrons* because pilgrims gather in the name of the patron saint of the well. Patterns often involve very complicated rituals with special numbers and directions. In this case seven circuits each of the two wells, the bath houses (as one) and each of the seven cairns of stones have to be made, followed by seven cicuits of the whole site, making seventy-seven circuits in total. This is all sometimes done with the person on their knees. The penitent then sits on rocks known as St Patrick's chair, turning round three times sunwise (*left to right*). This direction is considered to be lucky.

The Irish people have a strong, continuing tradition of pilgrimage, as a journey of spiritual and religious reflection and renewal. At the *Tobar an Ailt*, in Sligo, pilgrims gather for Mass and to follow the Stations of the Cross on the last Sunday in July. This has its roots in the Celtic festival of Lughnasa, celebrating the first fruits of the harvest.

Ireland has many holy wells spread throughout the land. In the 1980s it was reckoned in thousands, and throughout the British Isles the number is enormous. The following gazetteer can therefore only represent a minute proportion of these beautiful and atmospheric locations.

GAZETTEER OF SELECTED HOLY WELLS

WITH OS MAP REFERENCES AND PAGE NUMBERS OF SITES MENTIONED OR ILLUSTRATED IN THE TEXT

ENGLAND

BEDFORDSHIRE: *Holy Well*, Stevington (TL991536) Near to church.

BERKSHIRE: *St Ann's Well*, Caversham, Reading. At the top of Priest Hill.

BUCKINGHAMSHIRE: *Schorne Well*, North Marston (SP777226) In centre of village, named after rector Dr John Schorne, who is famed for capturing the devil in a boot.

CAMBRIDGESHIRE: *Holy Well*, Holywell, St Ives (TL336707) Behind church.

CHESHIRE: *St Oswald's Well*, Winwick, Warrington [p.25] (SJ958942) Overgrown in field of Woodhead Farm, Hermitage Green. *St Plegmund's Well*, Plemstall, Mickle Trafford [p.25]. At left side of road on the way to St Peter's Church. Dry, but decorated. *Wizard's Well*, Alderley Edge [p.25, 26] (SJ858778) Off Alderley Edge to Macclesfield road, follow pathway marked to the Edge, turn left at the end.

CORNWALL: *Alsia Well*, St Buryan [p.8] (SW393251) Natural spring found tucked in a hollow, across a field. *Chapel Euny Well*, Sancreed [p.8] (SW399288) Near prehistoric village of Carn Euny. *Giant's Well*, St Michael's Mount [p.6] (SW515298) Also known as Jack the Giant Killer's Well, now covered. *Dupath Well*, Callington (SX374693) Largest well house in Cornwall, of stone and granite. *Madron Well*, Madron [p.2, 5, 6] (SW445327) Ruined baptistry, well and rag bush. *Nanceglos Well*, West Penrith [p.6] (SW452313) Situated near entrance to Trengwainton Gardens, in recess in wall. *Sancreed Well*, Sancreed [p.6]. (SW418293) Follow footpath opposite the church and descend steps to well. *St Ambrusca's Well* (St Ambrew's), Crantock [p.i] (SW789607) In hedge, kept locked, with carved face on door, exact replica of the original. *St Cleer's Well*, St Cleer [p.5] (SX249683) Enclosed in chapel, by Celtic Cross. Used as a bowsening pool to cure madness. *St Clethers Well*, St Clether (SX203847) Largest well chapel in Cornwall, restored late nineteenth century. Water flows through the chapel. *St Levan's Well*, Porthcurno [p.7, 8] (SW381219) On cliff, overlooking bay. In ruins. *St Nonna's Well*, Altarnun (SX226816) In field below village, was used as a bowsening pool to cure madness.

CUMBRIA: *St Cuthbert's Well*, Edenhall [p.30] (NY564321) In field overlooked by church, overgrown and inaccessible on private land. The Luck of Edenhall is on show in the V&A, London, (glass gallery, no. 131). *St Helen's Well*, Great Ashby [p.30] (NY682132) A baptismal and pilgrimage well in fair condition. *St Mungo's Well*, Caldbeck (NY325398) Behind St Kentigern's church, by river. *St Oswald's Well*, Kirkoswald [p.30, 31] (NY555408) Beside church. *St Patrick's Well*, Aspatria [p.30] (NY147418) Beneath church. *St Patrick's Well*, Patterdale [p.30] (NY388166) Abandoned well house beside the main road, at head of Ullswater.

DERBYSHIRE: *Sheepwash Well*, and pumps beside road at Ashford-in-the-Water [p.32]. *Peat Well* (293579), **Bath House Spring** (218686) both in Bakewell. *Mompesson's Well*, Eyam [p.32] (SK222772) north of village, used as an exchange point for food and money at the time of the Great Plague. *St Ann's Well*, Buxton [p.32, 33, 34] (057735) Well building occasionally accessible at the bottom of the Slopes, and outdoor fountain nearby. *Thermal springs* at

Stoney Middleton [p.32] (232756). **Coffin Well** *[p.35] (177522)*, **Hall Well** *(176523)*, **Hands Well** *(178523)*, **Town Well** *(175524)*, **Yew Tree Well** *(174525)* and the **Children's Well** - *all around Tissington [p.32, 34].*

DEVON: *St Martin's Well*, *Cathedral Close, Exeter. Roman well.* **St Nectan's Well**, *Stoke, nr. Hartland (SS236247) Off main street, stone building.* **St Nectan's Well**, *Welcombe (SS228184) Near church.*

DORSET: *Holy Well*, *Holwell, nr Sherborne (ST699121) Near to St Lawrence's church.* **St Augustine's Well**, *Cerne Abbas [p.10, 11] (ST665016) Near the abbey.* **St Candida's Well** *(St Wite's), Morcombelake [p.2, 10]. On Chardown Hill, one mile south of the church of St Candida and Holy Cross at Whitchurch Canonicorum, now decayed and rises in a stone cattle trough.* **Wishing Well**, *Upwey [p.10] (SY661852) Near church.*

GLOUCESTERSHIRE: *Cheltenham. Spa town [p.24].* **Lady's Well**, *Hempstead [p.18] (SO815173) Near to the church of St Swithun.* **St Anthony's Well**, *near Micheldean [p.18]. Follow the Flaxley Brook to its source.* **Seven Wells**, *Bisley [p.18, 19] (SO903059) Attractive well house below church, and see also the unusual well cross in the churchyard, known as the 'Bonehouse'.*

HEREFORD AND WORCESTER: *Droitwich. Spa town, with modern Brine Bath open to the public.* **Holy Well**, *Malvern Wells [p.22, 23, 24] (SO770423) Unusual building.* **St Ann's Well**, *Great Malvern [p.22] (SO772458) Steep climb from Great Malvern.* **St Ethelbert's Well**, *Hereford [p.22]. Near entrance to Castle Green.* **St Ethelbert's Well**, *Marden [p.22] (SO512471) Covered well inside church.* **St Kenelm's Well**, *Romsley, Clent Hills [p.22] (SO945808) Near church.*

HUMBERSIDE: *St John's Well*, *Harpham (TA095617) Just outside village, follow land east from Crossgates.*

ISLE OF MAN: *St Maughold's Well*, *Maughold Head. Half a mile from village of Maughold. The spring rose where the saint's horse landed.*

KENT: *Royal Tunbridge Wells. Spa town [p.24].* **St Edith's Well**, *Kemsing, near Sevenoakes. In centre of village, once situated in the gardens of a convent.*

LANCASHIRE: *St Patrick's Well*, *Heysham [p.iii, 28]. Near entrance to St Peter's church, set in wall, now dry.* **Hic-bibi Well**, *Coppull [p.28]. Follow footpath at the end of Hic-bibi Lane. A sign marks the well.* **Ladyewell**, *Fernhalgh, near Broughton [p.28, 29] (SD555340) Not marked on map, but worth the search.* **Peg o' Nell's Well**, *Bungerley Bridge, near Clitheroe [p.2]. In grounds of Waddow Hall.* **St Michael's Well**, *Bolton-le-Sands [p.iv, 28]. In St Michael's Lane, a clear, bubbling spring.* **Standish Well**, *Standish [p.28]. By church. Restored, but dry.*

LONDON: *St Mary's Well*, *Willesden [p.40]. Rising in pump inside parish church. See also the pilgrimage statue of the Black Virgin [p.41].* **Well Walk**, *Hampstead [p.40]. Nineteenth century fountain situated on the site of the famous Hampstead Spa.*

NORFOLK: *Holy Well*, *Anglican Shrine, Little Walsingham. In centre of village.* **Holy Wells**, *Little Walsingham [p.38, 39]. In centre of village in the abbey grounds.* **St Walstan's Well**, *Bawburgh [p.38]. In farmyard near church, looks like a story book well but was once a great pilgrimage site.* **St Withburga's Well**, *East Dereham [p.38] (TF986134) In churchyard of St Nicholas' church.*

NORTHAMPTONSHIRE: *Becket's Well*, *Northampton (SP761602) On Bedford Road.*

NORTHUMBERLAND: *Coventina's Well*, *Carrawburgh [p.1]. Roman temple complex.* **Lady's Well**, *Holystone (NT953029) To the north of village.* **St Cuthbert's Well**, *Bellingham (NY837833) Outside churchyard.*

NOTTINGHAMSHIRE: *Holy Well*, Watnall (499456) Eight miles NW of Nottingham. *St Catherine's Well*, Newark. Just outside Newark, the site is marked.

OXFORDSHIRE: *Fair Rosamond's Well*, Blenheim Park [p.20] (SP436164) On north bank of Blenheim Lake. Park Admission charge. *St Bartholomew's Well*, Cowley, Oxford [p.20]. In churchyard. *St Margaret's Well*, Binsey [p.20, 21] (SP486080) In churchyard. **The Lady's Well**, Wilcote, Finstock [p.20] (SP374148) In Wychwood Forest.

SHROPSHIRE: *St Cuthbert's Well*, Donington (SJ808045) Below church. *St Winifred's Well*, Woolston (SJ322244) Half timbered building over water.

SOMERSET: *Chalice Well*, Glastonbury [p.12, 13] (ST507385) Below Glastonbury Tor, in Chalice Well gardens. Admission charge. *Holy Well*, Frome (ST777479) By the parish church. *Hot Springs*, Roman Bath and Museum, Bath [p.14, 15, 24]. In centre of Bath. Admission charge. *St Aldhelm's Well*, Doulting [p.12, 16] (ST647432) Near church. *St Andrew's Well*, Stogursey (ST203428) In centre of village. *St Andrew's Well*, Wells [p.12]. Flows from under cathedral to city cross, conduit open to view in cloisters. *St Joseph's Well*, Glastonbury Abbey, Glastonbury. In niche, in the south wall of the Lady Chapel.

STAFFORDSHIRE: *Egg Well*, Bradnop (SK006541) One mile south of the village. *St Chad's Well*, Stowe, Lichfield [p.16] (SK122103) In churchyard behind the church.

SUFFOLK: *Lady Well*, Woolpit. Eleven miles east of Bury St Edmunds. Spring on far side of A45, used for healing eyes.

SURREY: *St Mary the Virgin's Well*, Dunsfold (SU997363) Near church, with oak canopy.

WARWICKSHIRE: *Holy Well*, Burton Dassett (SP398515) On left side of road approaching church. **Royal Leamington Spa**. Spa town [p.24].

WILTSHIRE: *Conkwell*, Winsley [p.14] (ST791626) In the hamlet of Conkwell. **Daniel's Well**, Malmesbury [p.16] (ST931871) Situated below the Abbey. Spring flowing into pool. **Dipping Well**, Market Lavington [p.16] (SU016540) In centre of the village, by playground. **Holt**, remains of Spa house entrance. **Monk's Well**, Edington [p.vi, 16] (ST924530) Found off the main road at Bratton end of village, on right of way over private land. **Monk's Well**, Monkton Farleigh [p.14] (ST803656) North of village, the well house supplied the Cluniac priory of St Mary Magdalene. **Swallowhead Spring**, Avebury [p.16, 17] (101681) Source of River Kennet, near Silbury Hill. Dry in the autumn and winter, it flows again in late winter for the return of spring.

YORKSHIRE: *Harrogate*. Spa town [p.24]. **Robin Hood's Well**, Fountains Abbey (SE276683) On footpath by south bank of River Skell. *St Cedd's Well*, Lastingham [p.36] (SE739904) Near church, by bridge, and *St Chad's Well*, Lastingham [p.36]. Dry, near St Cedd's Well. *St Hilda's Well*, Hinderwell [pg 36, 37] (NZ791170) In churchyard. *St John's Well*, Mount Grace Priory, Northallerton (SE449983) Short distance from southeast corner of Priory. **The Ebbing and Flowing Well**, Giggleswick [p.36] (SO805654) Near St Alkeda's church, northeast of Giggleswick. **The Dropping Well**, Knaresborough [p.36] (SE348565) Example of a petrifying well, where the limestone content of the water solidifies objects. By Mother Shipton's cave. Admission charge.

WALES

ANGLESEY: *St Seiriol's Well*, Penmon [p.1, 44] (SH631808) Near Penmon Priory, under cliff.

DYFED: *St Anthony's Well*, Llanstephan, near Carmarthen [p.42]. On cliff. *St Govan's Well*, St Govan's Head, [p.10, 42, **43**] near Bosherston (9792) Chapel in crevice by well, now dry. Occasionally inaccessible due to military training. *St Mary's Well*, Maenclochog [p.42] (SN076271) To west of village. *St Non's Well*, St Davids [p.42] (SM751243). Chapel and well off land leading to St Non's Bay.

CLWYD: *St Beuno's Well*, Tremeirchon [p.46] (SJ083723) In the front garden of Ffynnon Beuno cottage. *St Dyfnog's Well*, Lllanrhaeadr [p.46]. (SJ081633) In wood behind church, follow stream right to find large bathing pool. *St Winefride's Well*, Holywell [p.2, 47] (SJ185763) Below church. Small admission charge.

GOWER: *Holy Well*, Cefn Bryn (555489) Situated 500 metres from Arthur's Stone, a burial chamber which tradition says has an ebbing and flowing well beneath it used for making wishes.

GWENT: *Holy Well*, Sudbrook (ST5288) Remains seen by ruins of St Tecia's Chapel. Visit at low tide, on island. *Virtuous Well*, Trellech (SO5005) To the north of Llandogo road.

GWYNEDD: *Beuno's Well*, Clynnog Fawr [p.44]. Near church. *St Celynin's Holy Well*, Llangelynin, near Henryd [p.46] (SH751738) In isolated location above Conwy valley. *St Cybi's Well*, Llangybi [p.44, **45**] (SH427413) Through churchyard, down into valley.

POWYS: *Llandrindod Wells*. Spa town [p.24]. Pump room in Rock Park. *St Myllin's Well*, Llanfyllin. Above town on hillside. Restored.

SCOTLAND

ABERDEEN: *St Drostan's Well*, New Aberdour (NJ887646) On shore, down cliff road.

ARGYLL: *Barbeek Well*, Barbreek (NM824062) Stone lined tank, now wishing well. *St Cairrell's Well*, Creagan (NM980450) On track near Loch Creran.

BANFF: *St Fumac's Well*, Botriphnie. In manse garden by churchyard. *St Michael's Well*, Kirkmichael [p.44]. By parish church.

DUNBARTON: *St Ronan's Well* (St Marnock's), Kilmaronock Castle (NS448877) Near church adjoining castle.

EDINBURGH: *St Margaret's Well*, Holyrood Park [p.48]. Near ruins of St Anthony's chapel.

FIFE: *Holy Well*, Auchtertool (NT208902) South of village by kirk. *St Fillan's Well*, Aberdour [p.48] (NT194854) Southeast of old churchyard. *St Fillan's Well*, Pittenweem [p.48]. Through doorway into cave at Cove Wynd. *St Theriot's Well*, Fordell (NT147853) In Fordell Castle grounds.

GLASGOW: *St Mungo's Well*, in Glasgow cathedral.

GRAMPIAN: *Burghead Holy Well*, Burghead [p.50] (NJ109692) In continuation of King Street, off Church Street.

INVERNESS: *St Ignatius' Well*, Glassburn [p.50]. On A831. *St Mary's Well*, Culloden [p.50] (NH723453) In Culloden Wood. *Well of the Heads*, Invergarry [p.50, **51**] (NN304993) On road by Loch Oich.

KINCARDINE: *St Caran's Well* (Kieran's), Stonehaven (NO868868) Near distillery, below Glenury railway viaduct.

KINROSS: *Scotlandwell*, Scotlandwell [p.48, **49**] (NO185016) In centre of village.

KIRKCUDBRIGHT: *Glebe Well*, Kirkbean. On hillside, above village. *Holy Well*, Parton. On A713, north of Castle Douglas. *Rutherford's Well*, Anwoth (NX584562) Behind ruins of old church. *St Queran's Well* (Jergon's), Troqueer (NX957722)

LANARK: *St Patrick's Well*, Lanark (NS875437) *On south side of main street.*

LOTHIAN: *Brand's Well*, Gullane. (NT476816) *Near A198.* *Cross Well*, Linlithgow. *South of Palace, in square.* *Holy Well*, Spott (NT6775) *Near churchyard. Now dry.* *Our Lady's Well*, Stow. *Half a mile south of Stow church. Well by chapel.* *Our Lady's Well*, Whitekirk (NT598816) *Off A198, north east of village.* *Rood Well*, Stenton (NT624744) *By side of B6370.* *St Baldred's Well*, East Linton (NT593779) *Across road from graveyard of parish church of Preston.*

ROSS AND CROMARTY: *Craiguck Well* (or Craigie), Avoch (NH679532) *On north shore Munlochy bay.* *Cloutie Well* (St Boniface's Well), Munlochy [p.50] (NH641537) *On A832 to Tore.* *Strathpeffer.* *Spa town [p.24].*

SELKIRK: *Mungo's Well*, Selkirk (NT473280) *In Haining Deer Park.*

WIGTOWN: *St Finnan's Well*, Mochrum (NX278490) *By side of A747, in ruined St Finnan's Chapel.* *Well of the Rees*, Kirkcowan (NX229724) *Quarter of a mile north of Kilgallioch, near site of old church.*

IRELAND

ANTRIM: *St Colman's Well*, Churchtown, near Randalstown. *By Lough Neagh, near church.*

ARMAGH: *Holy Well*, Coney Island, on Lough Neagh.

CARLOW: *St Moling's Well*, St Mullins (S73 38) *150 yards north of monastery.*

CLARE: *St Brigid's Well*, Liscannor. *Two and a half miles northwest, near nineteenth century monument.* *St Mac Creiche's Well*, Liscannor. *One mile north of village, on seashore near church.*

CORK: *St Olann's Well*, Coolineagh, near Coachford (W44 78) *North northeast of church.*

DONEGAL: *Doon Well*, Kilmacrenan (C12 20) *Southeast of Doon Rock.* *Malin Well*, Malin Head. *Natural rock basin of fresh water, covered at high tide.*

DOWN: *Struel Wells* (St Patrick's Wells), Downpatrick [p.16, 52, 53]. *Mearing Well*, Saul. *Near church.*

DUBLIN: *Lady Well*, Mulhuddart. *Southwest of church.*

FERMANAGH: *St Patrick's Well*, Holywell village, northwest of Belcoo.

KERRY: *St Molaga's Well*, Ballineanig near Ballyferriter (Q35 03) *East of ruined oratory.* *St Manchán's Well*, Ballymoreagh, west of Dingle (Q40 02) *By oratory.*

LOUGH: *St Brigid's Well*, Faughart, near Dundalk. *In churchyard.*

MAYO: *St Columcille's Well*, Oughval. *Beside ancient church.*

MEATH: *St Ciarán's Well*, Castlekeeran, near Kells. *By churchyard.*

OFFALY: *St Ciarán's Well*, Clonmacnoise (N01 31) *By Shannonbridge road, west of cemetery.* *St Manchán's Well*, Lemanaghan, Ferbane (N17 27) *East of church.*

ROSCOMMON: *Bride's Well*, Brideswell (M94 44). *Lassair Well*, Kilronan. *On Loch Mealey, near church ruins.*

SLIGO: *Tobar an Ailt*, three miles from Sligo town, on shore of Lough Gill.

WATERFORD: *St Declan's Well*, Ardmore (X19 77) *Southeast of village.*

WESTMEATH: *St Féchin's Well*, Fore. *By ancient church.*

WEXFORD: *St Mogue's Well*, Ferns (T01 50) *Outside graveyard.*